Coloring Book Love
Mandalas
Volume 1

K.S. PIERCE

ISBN: 978-0-692-51702-4
First Edition: August 2015

SHARE YOUR CREATIONS WITH US!

Want to have your color artwork featured
on our social media pages?
Then be sure to tag your pictures
#coloringbooklove or #coloringbookluv

Sign up to get free coloring pages
and a chance to win in our giveaways!

www.ColoringBookLove.com

Welcome to the Coloring Book Love Mandalas Volume 1!

In this volume, I encourage you to turn the pages and start your coloring journey with 50 Mandalas with varying shapes and patterns. This coloring book showcases both hand-drawn and computer generated images. Go on a creative adventure and start your relaxation, meditation, manifestation, creative expression, inspiration, self-discovery and healing all from the comfort of your favorite corner or spot to color.

Mandalas represent wholeness and are perfect for decorating with all kinds of mediums - color pencils, crayons, markers, gel pens, or watercolors, among others.

Coloring these Mandalas is a unique method of visual self expression. You may experience a feeling of relief, a sense of peace as the pattern comes together within the circle. They are not only beautiful with intricate patterns or designs, they are also powerful tools for inspiration, self-discovery and healing.

It is my ardent hope that as you flip through the pages of this coloring book and start coloring you find yourself being freed from whatever worries, stresses or negativities pulling you down. It's about time. You deserve it.

Happy coloring!
K.S. Pierce

You're never too old (or too young) to color!

Here's what to do next:

1. Find a comfortable place where you can color. This coloring book is created precisely so you can enjoy the process.

2. If you would like to make several versions of your artwork, or are afraid you might make mistakes, make sure to make a copy of the page. This will also give you the chance to select your preferred paper (thicker and won't bleed) ready for framing.

3. Please note that if you are using markers or gel pens, consider using scrap paper behind the page you're coloring to prevent bleed-through.

4. Use your favorite medium or a combination of mediums. Break out your favorite coloring pencils, coloring markers, gel pens, crayons, etc., and start your coloring journey!

5. Most important of all - Be yourself, express yourself! Remember, there is no wrong way, or right way to paint or color. Whatever you decide to do with these pages, the result will be unique and beautiful!

6. Once you're done with your creations, share them with the world! You may display them or give them as gifts.

7. It's time for your relaxation, meditation, manifestation, creative expression, inspiration, self-discovery and healing. Let's begin!

Good Things Are Going To Happen.
Have Faith. Stay Positive.

Failure will never overtake me
if my determination to succeed is strong enough.

– Og Mandino

Your talent is God's gift to you.
What you do with it is your gift back to God.
- Leo Buscalgia

You are never too old
to set another goal or to dream a new dream.
- C.S. Lewis

A goal is a dream with a deadline
- Napoleon Hill

A creative man is motivated by the desire to achieve,
not by the desire to beat others.
- Ayn Rand

With the new day comes
new strength and new thoughts.
– Eleanor Roosevelt

It does not matter how slowly you go
as long as you do not stop.
- Confucius

Don't watch the clock;
do what it does.
Keep going.
- Sam Levenson

Infuse your life with action. Don't wait for it to happen.
Make it happen.
Make your own future.
Make your own hope.
Make your own love.
And whatever your beliefs, honor your Creator,
not by passively waiting for grace to come down from upon high,
but by doing what you can to make grace happen...
yourself, right now, right down here on Earth.
- Bradley Whitford

Believe in yourself!
Have faith in your abilities!
Without a humble but reasonable
confidence in your own powers
you cannot be successful or happy.
- Norman Vincent Peale

If you can dream it,
you can do it.
- Walt Disney

You have to learn the rules of the game.
And then you have to
play better than anyone else.
- Albert Einstein

The will to win, the desire to succeed,
the urge to reach your full potential...
these are the keys that will unlock
the door to personal excellence.
- Confucius

Problems are not stop signs,
they are guidelines.
- Robert H. Schuller

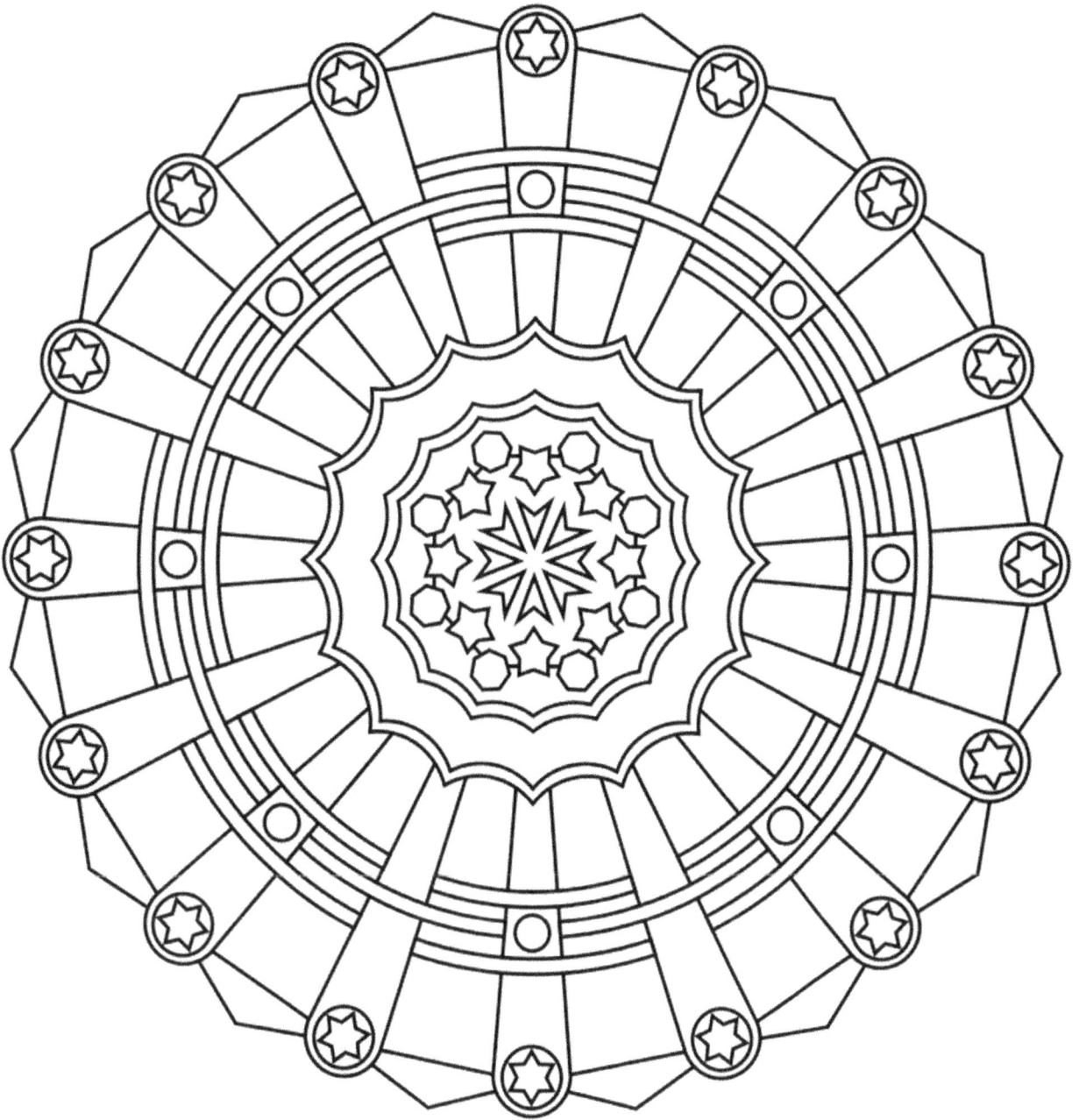

The secret of getting ahead
is getting started.
- Mark Twain

There is only one corner of the universe
you can be certain of improving,
and that's your own self.
- Aldous Huxley

Expect problems
and eat them for breakfast.
- Alfred A. Montapert

We may encounter many defeats
but we must not be defeated.
- Maya Angelou

Things do not happen.
Things are made to happen.
- John F. Kennedy

Start where you are.
Use what you have.
Do what you can.
- Arthur Ashe

Be kind whenever possible.
It is always possible.
- Dalai Lama

Never give up,
for that is just the place and time
that the tide will turn.
- Harriet Beecher Stowe

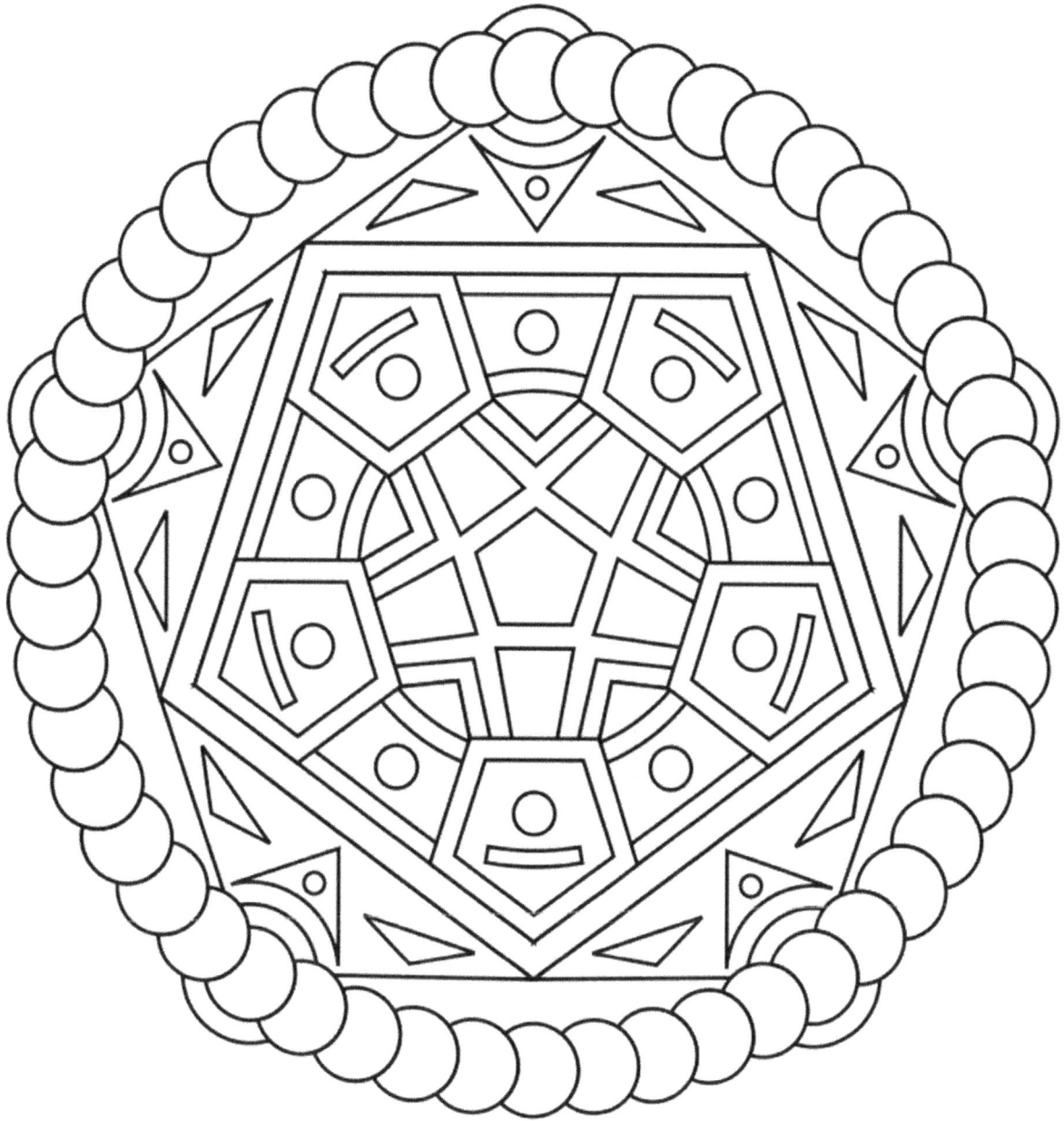

Accept the challenges
so that you can feel
the exhilaration of victory.
- George S. Patton

Optimism is the faith
that leads to achievement.
Nothing can be done
without hope and confidence.
- Helen Keller

Beginning today,
treat everyone you meet as if they were
going to be dead by midnight.
Extend to them all the
care, kindness and understanding
you can muster,
and do it with no thought of any reward.
Your life will never be the same again.
- Og Mandino

The key is to keep company
only with people who uplift you,
whose presence calls forth your best.
- Epictetus

Ever tried.
Ever failed.
No matter.
Try again.
Fail again.
Fail better.
- Samuel Beckett

What you get by achieving your goals
is not as important as what you become
by achieving your goals.
- Zig Ziglar

Setting goals is the first step
in turning the invisible into the visible.
- Tony Robbins

Do you want to know who you are?
Don't ask. Act!
Action will delineate and define you.
- Thomas Jefferson

Even if you fall on your face,
you're still moving forward.
- Victor Kiam

Do the difficult things while they are easy
and do the great things while they are small.
A journey of a thousand miles
must begin with a single step.
- Lao Tzu

Consult not your fears
but your hopes and dreams.
Think not about your frustrations,
but about your unfulfilled potential.
Concern yourself not with what
you tried and failed in,
but with what it is still possible for you to do.
- Pope John XXIII

Perseverance is failing 19 times
and succeeding the 20th.
- Julie Andrews

Either I will find a way,
or I will make one.
- Philip Sidney

Do the one thing you think you cannot do.
Fail at it. Try again. Do better the second time.
The only people who never tumble
are those who never mount the high wire.
This is your moment. Own it.
- Oprah Winfrey

If you don't like something, change it.
If you cannot change it, change your attitude.
Don't complain.
- Maya Angelou

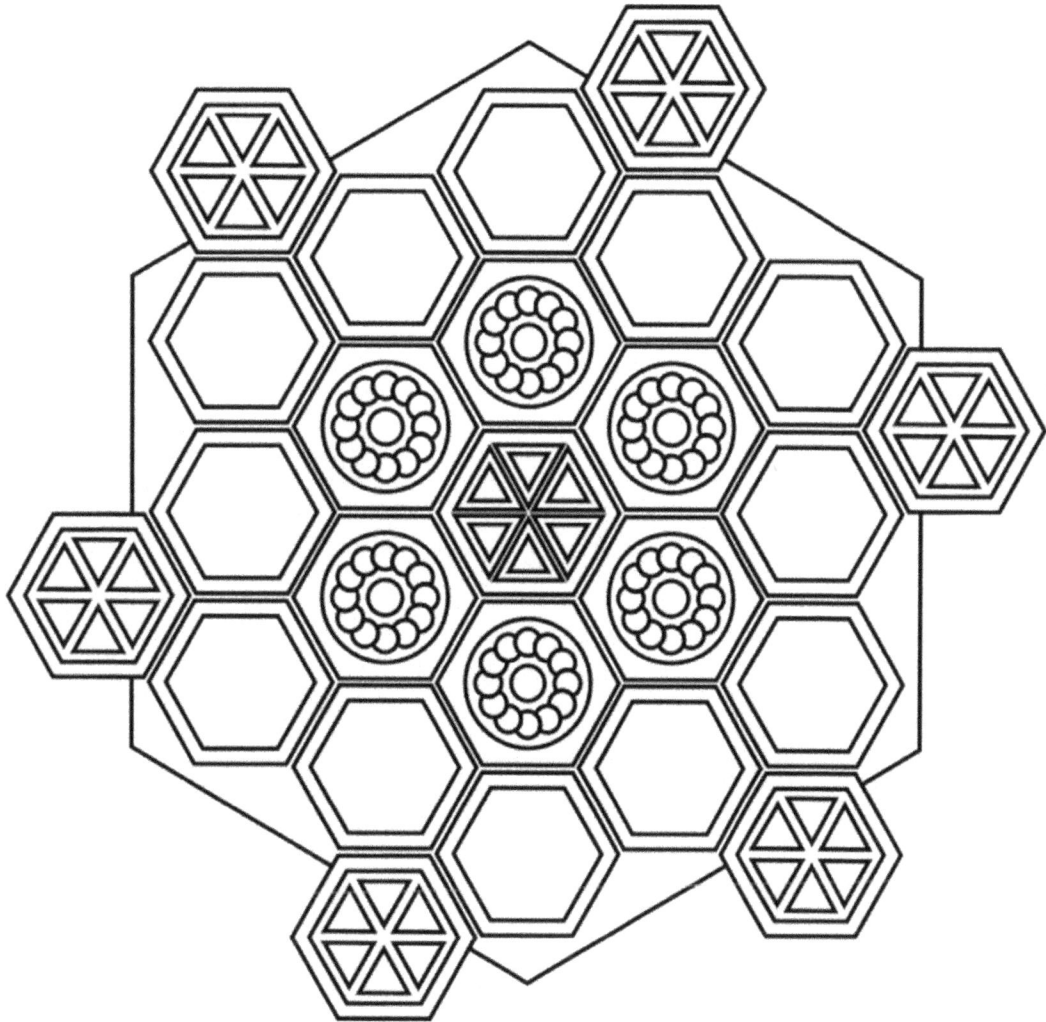

Don't give up.
Don't lose hope.
Don't sell out.
- Christopher Reeve

If you can dream it, then you can achieve it.
You will get all you want in life
if you help enough other people get what they want.
- Zig Ziglar

The past has no power
over the present moment.
- Eckhart Tolle

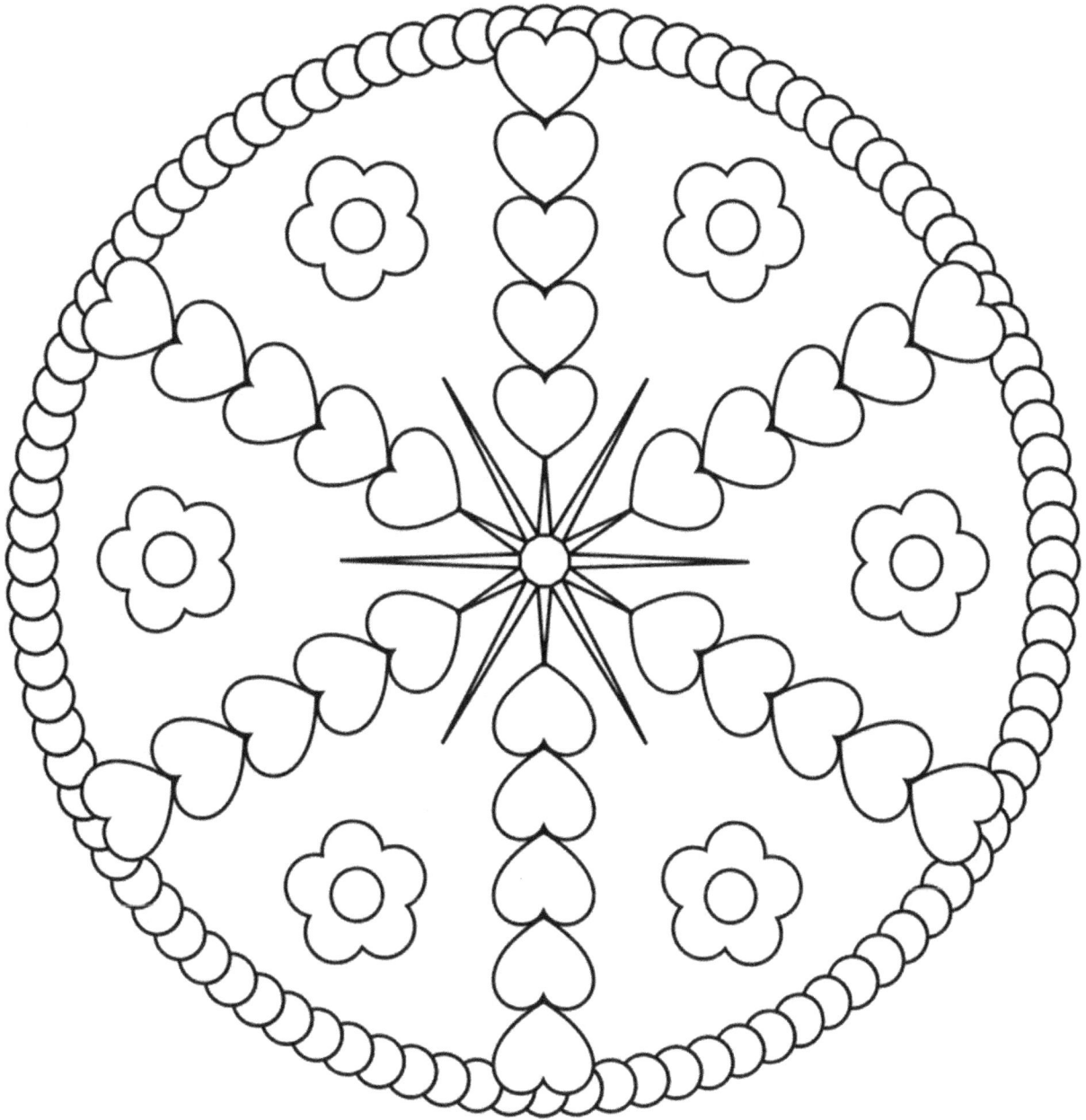

Life is a gift, and it offers us the
privilege, opportunity, and responsibility
to give something back by becoming more.
- Tony Robbins

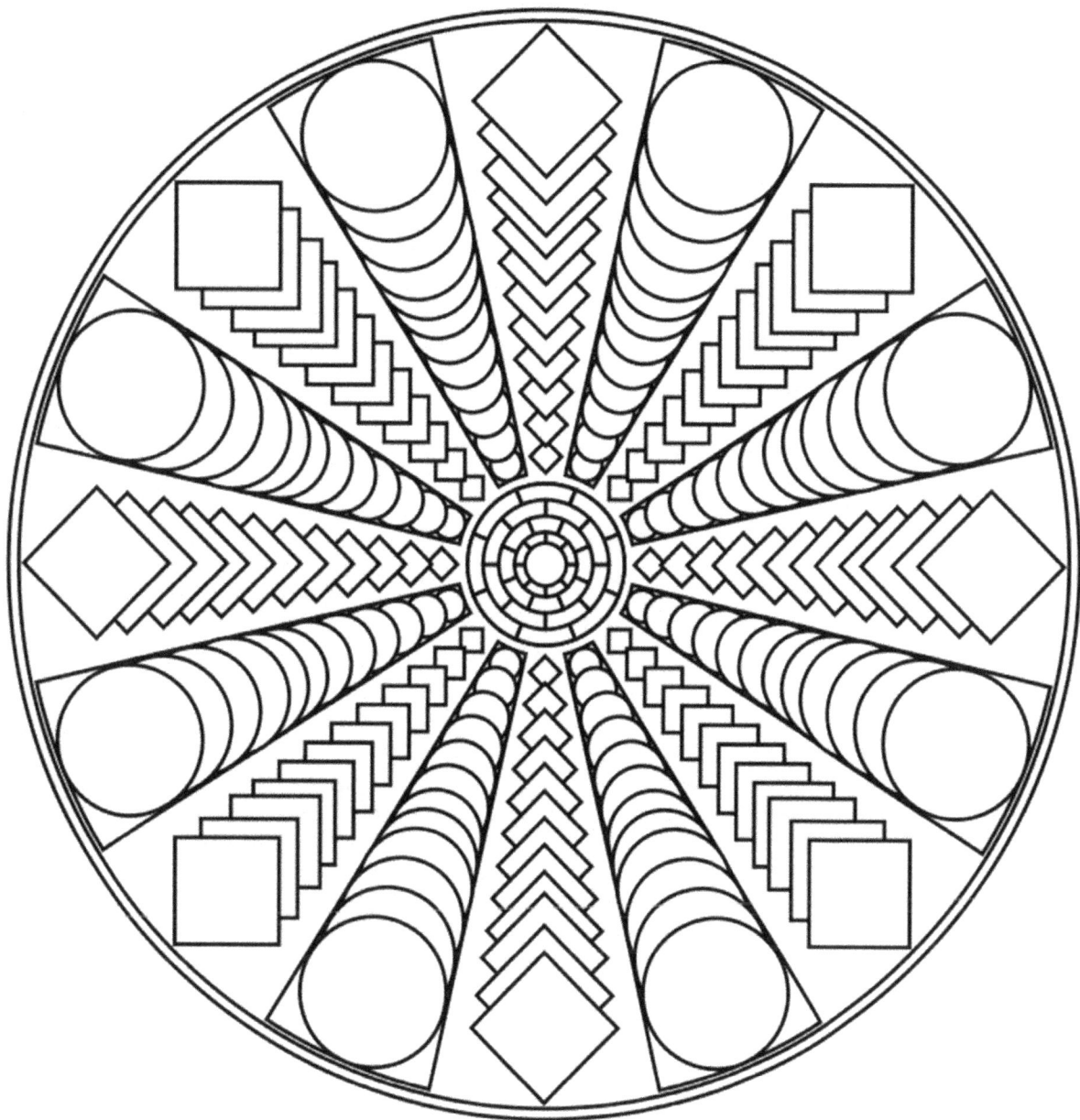

I am the greatest,
I said that even before I knew I was.
- Muhammad Ali

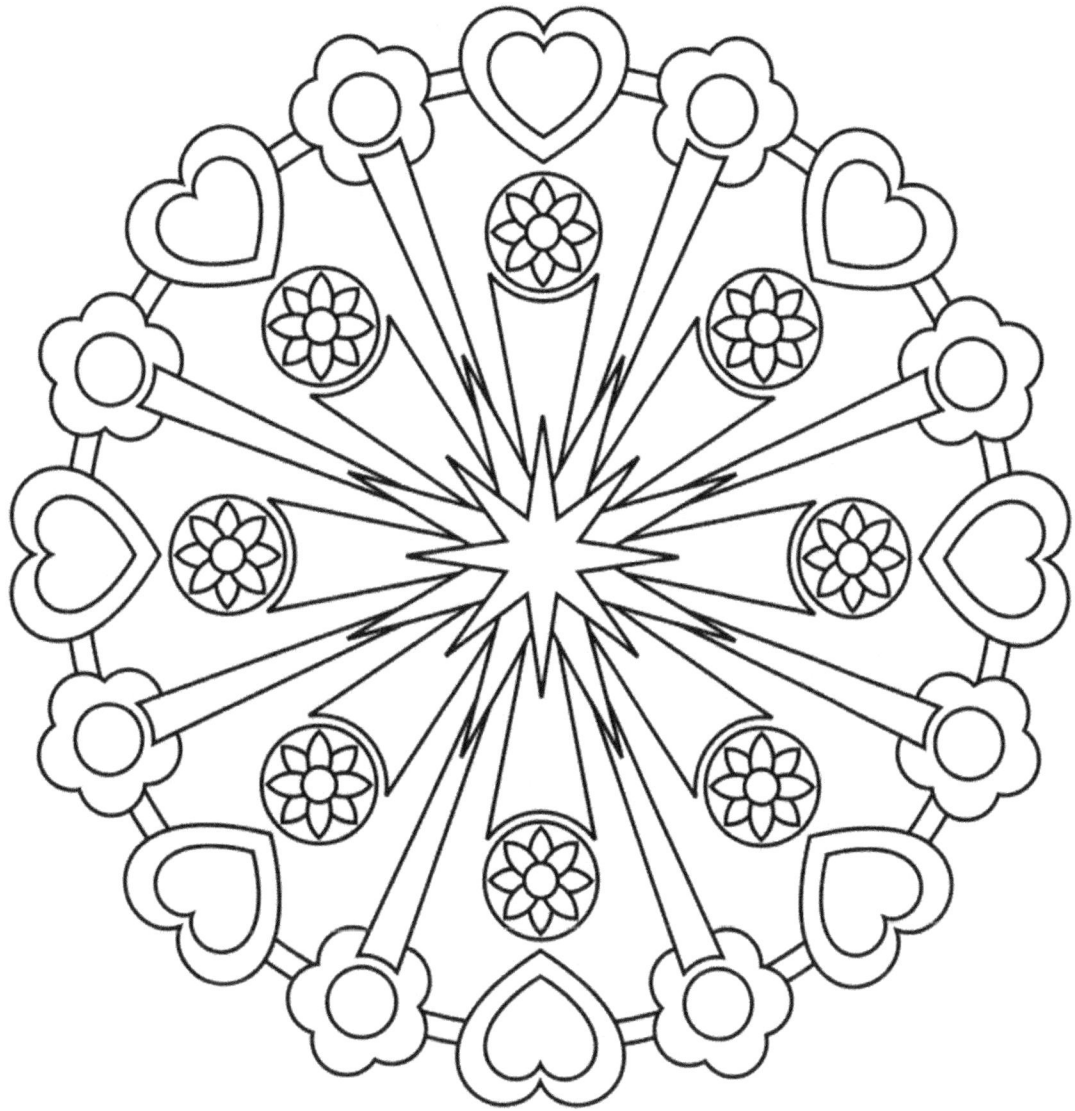

Be soft. Do not let the world make you hard.
Do not let pain make you hate.
Do not let the bitterness steal your sweetness.
Take pride that even though the rest of the world may disagree,
you still believe it to be a beautiful place.
- Kurt Vonnegut

Today is a new beginning,
a chance to turn your failures into achievements
& your sorrows into so goods.
No room for excuses.
- Joel Brown

When you are tempted to give up,
your breakthrough is probably just around the corner.
- Joyce Meyer

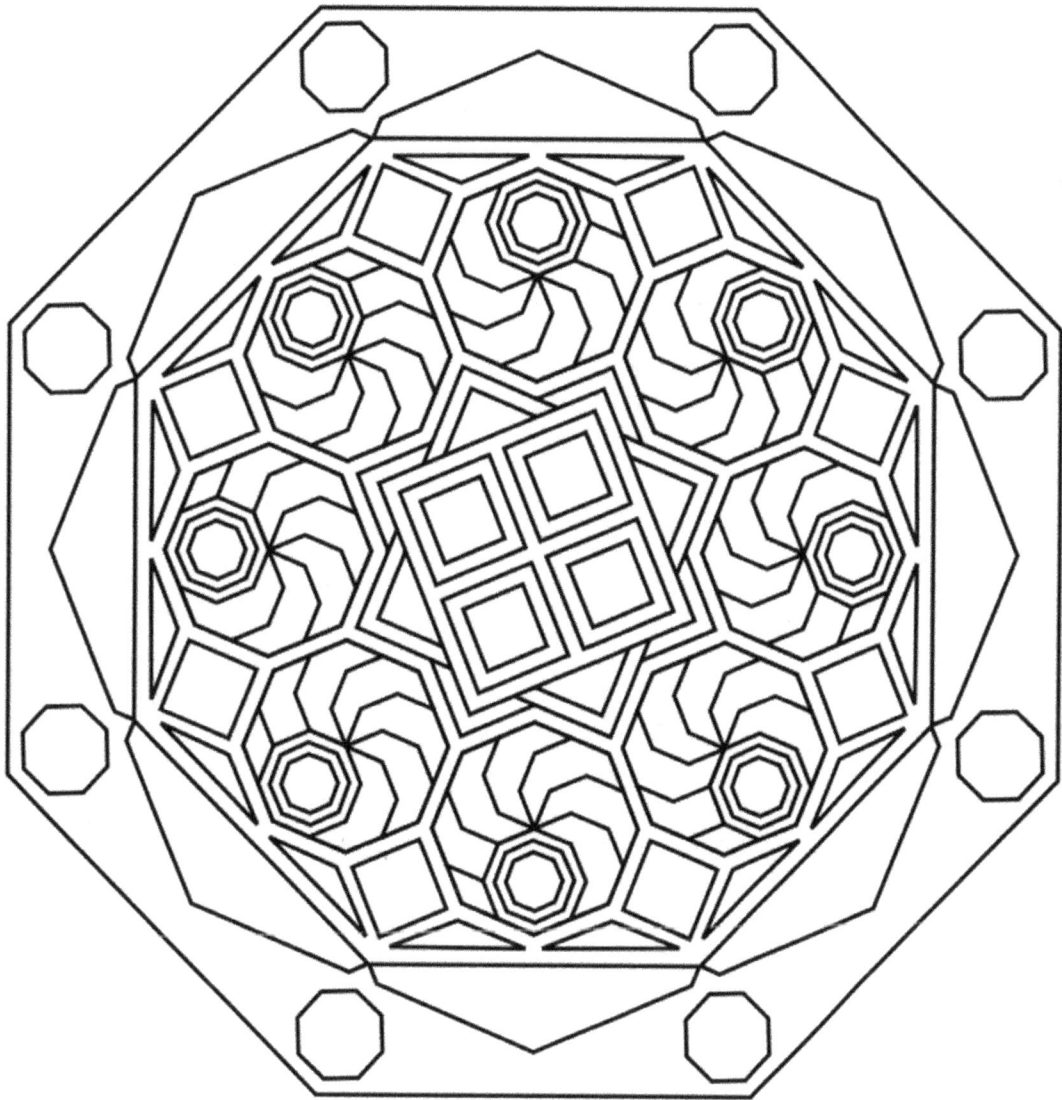

Take the first step in faith.
You don't have to see the whole staircase.
Just take the first step.
- Dr. Martin Luther King Jr.

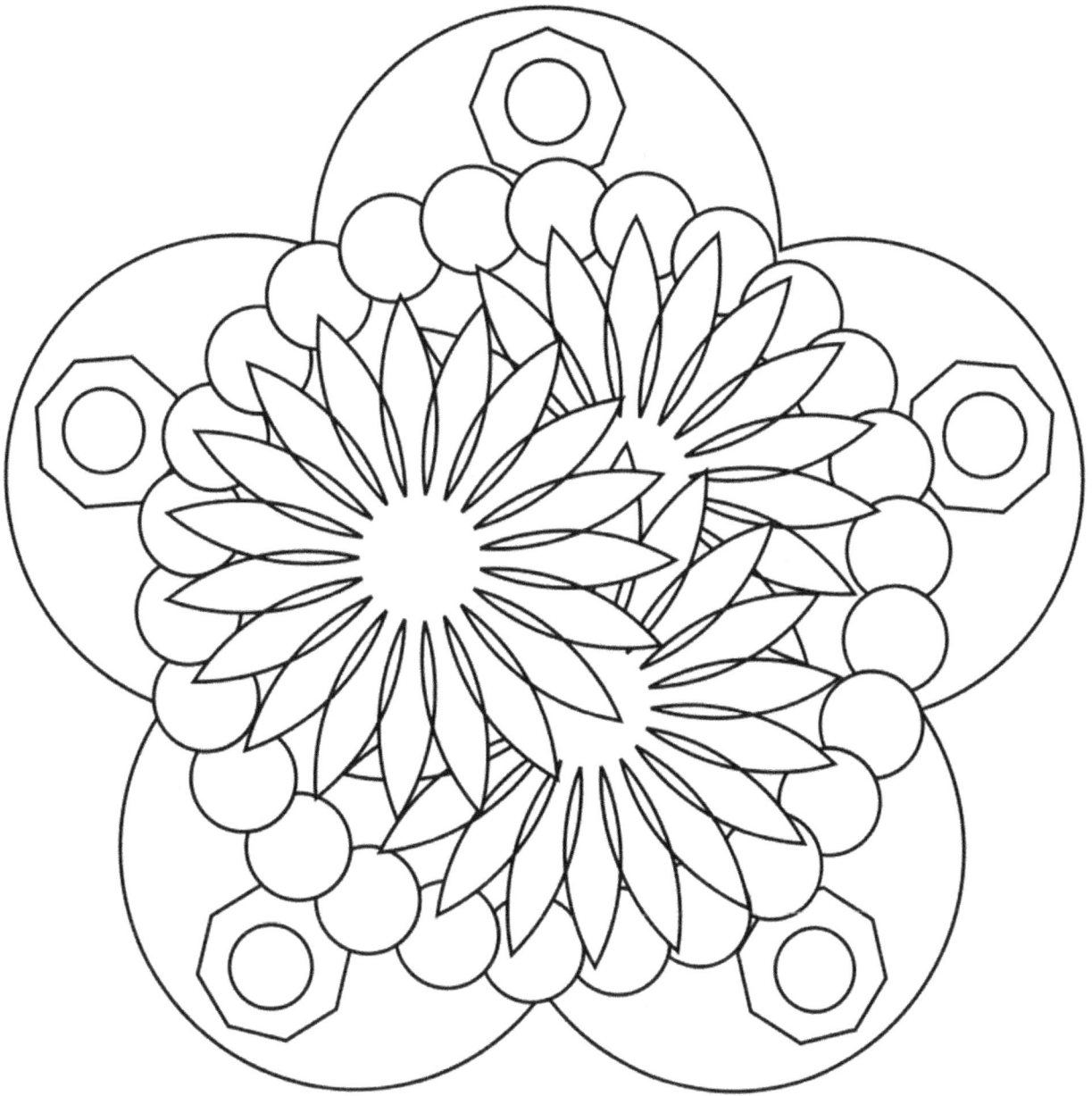

Imagination is everything.
It is the preview of life's coming attractions.
- Albert Einstein

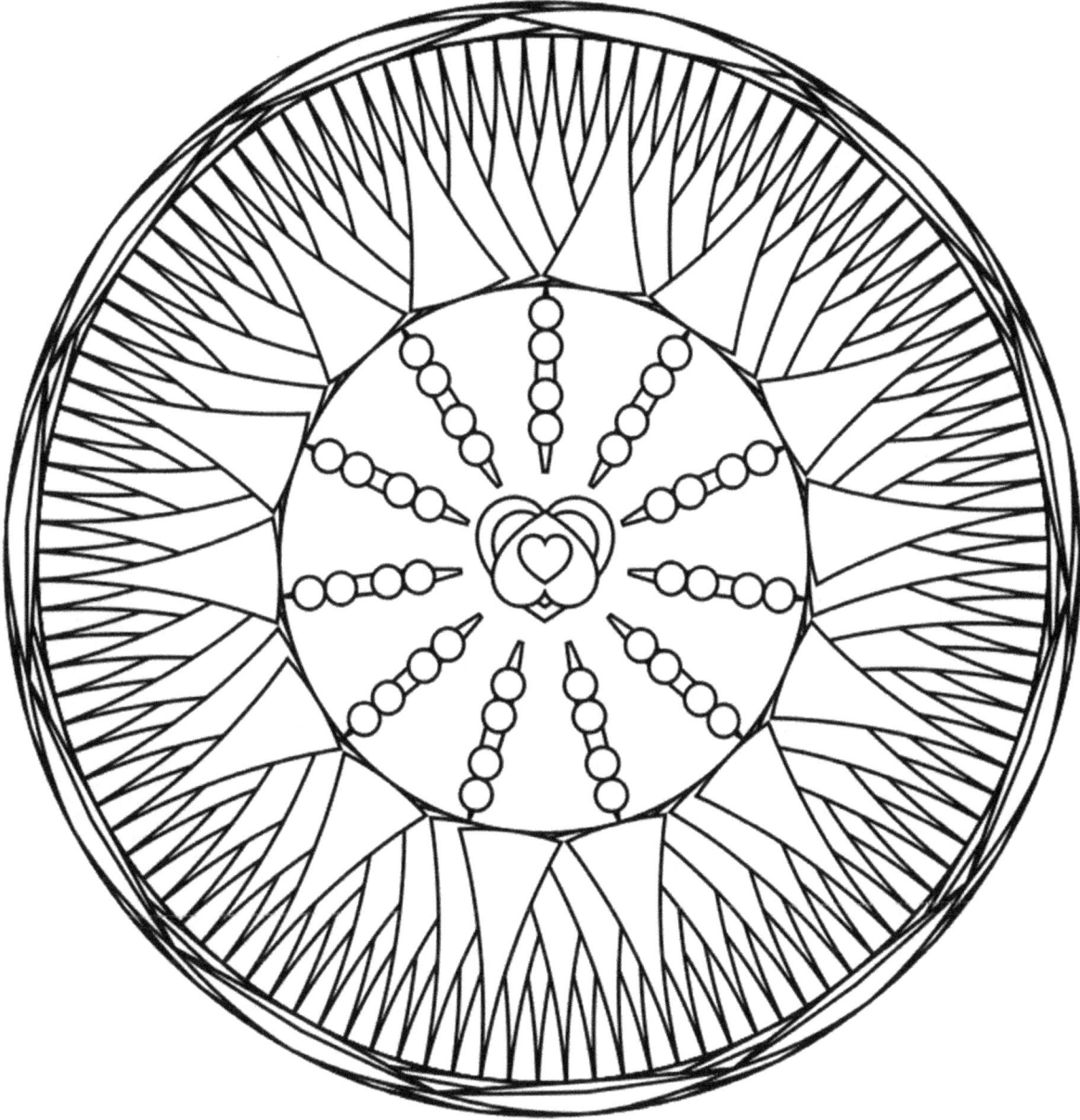

Gratitude is an attitude
that hooks us up to our source of supply.
And the more grateful you are,
the closer you become to your maker,
to the architect of the universe,
to the spiritual core of your being.
It's a phenomenal lesson.
- Bob Proctor

When life seems to be throwing too many curveballs
or you feel like you're not getting anything right -
remind yourself to be grateful for your life,
forgive your flaws, harness positive thinking,
banish limiting beliefs, think abundant thoughts
and always act on inspired actions.
You don't merely exist. You're not just a number.
Be proud of yourself for your resilience.
Be strong, brave, and beautiful.
Refuse to give up! You are an inspiration!
- Kristine Pierce

SHARE YOUR CREATIONS WITH US!

FACEBOOK.COM/
COLORINGBOOKLOVE

@ColoringBookLove

@ColoringBookLuv

@ColoringBookLuv

Want to have your color artwork featured

on our social media pages?

Then be sure to tag your pictures

#coloringbooklove or #coloringbookluv

Sign up to get free coloring pages

and a chance to win in our giveaways!

www.ColoringBookLove.com